A Near Death Experience:

I Died and Came Back From Hell

By Grady Mosby

PRESS

Join me on Facebook at A Near Death Experience:
I Died and Came Back from Hell

Write me at my Email address
andexperience@hotmail.com

www.xulonpress.com

Table of Contents

Introduction.. ix

Dedication xi

Acknowledgments... xiii

Chapter 1—Knowing.......................................15

Chapter 2—Beginning 21

Chapter 3—College bound 31

Chapter 4—Graduation....................................35

Chapter 5—Geographical 40

Chapter 6—First Death-Heaven 44

Chapter 7—Extradition....................................49

Chapter 8—Doing good/Doing bad 52

Chapter 9—Second Death-Hell 57

Chapter 10—Busted..63

Chapter 11—Desperation..................................68

Chapter 12—Salvation/Rebirth........................74

Conclusion 83

Notes 87

Top Ten Reasons to Read this Book...............

10. I want you to!

9. It might give you an idea for your own book.

8. You or someone you know has experienced something similar.

7. It is a short story and a quick read and will count as your goal to read a book.

6. It has a "Near Death Experience" you've never heard of.

5. Your Mom would want you to!

4. It connects the supernatural with the natural.

3. It might bring you peace about a similar situation in your life experience.

2. It can bring back your hope when your hope has gone.

1. It might help SAVE YOUR LIFE or someone you know.

NEVER GIVE UP!!

Introduction

A "Near-Death Experience" is a true story highlighting one man's human life experience. A man just like you or anyone you may know. It shows the results of how we might handle the voids and losses in our lives, if not dealt with openly at the time of occurrence. It takes a raw look at our addictive behavior, drugs, alcohol, sex, anger, depression, suicide and how hurting others can fill the emptiness created by loss.

It is a good read for parents to help understand what to watch out for in their children's behavior. It can also help, and is very important for, people who have some type of addict in their lives and for the addict still suffering.

This journal only describes basic details of several pivotal episodes. There were hundreds more bad situations and interactions that aren't chronicled in this book. The cost financially was well over a million dollars and the cost relationally unable to be calculated.

This is a story about living, loving, failing and ultimate recovery. It includes intervention from Angels and demons. It will bring tears to your eyes, when reading a real suicide letter, and will also make you shudder from the sound of the life saving Voice yelling "Put your seatbelt on!"

This man's earthly experience was almost ended early

with death many times. A graphic description of his two "near-death" experiences, are included. Once he died and saw Heaven and the second time he died and saw hell.

Conclusion: Heaven and hell both exist. I know because I've been there and I made it back to tell you about it! We need to decide where we want to go before we die, before it's too late.

Dedication

This story is dedicated to my mother Sharon. She was always there for me when I fell down and hit bottom, and was kind and loving till I bounced back. I also owe my life to her twice. Once for giving birth to me and twice because she taught me about Jesus. When I was dead in my sins, I knew what to do to be born again.

This story is also dedicated to my loving wife Susan. When I hurt and betrayed her, over and over, she believed in me and loved me enough to stay.

Acknowledgments

Thank you to the Salvation Army Adult Rehabilitation Center for Men in Tucson, Arizona for providing a place for the fallen man, to pick himself up and learn how to live again.

Thank you to the Maricopa County Superior Court Drug Court Diversion Program. Thank you for all the people that make it work, and for giving the addict a chance to get clean and avoid felony prosecution.

Thank you to the Hon. Judge Susan Bolton, who listened, and gave me another chance to save my life, with the Salvation Army Adult Rehabilitation Program.

Thank you to the Maricopa County Probation and Parole Department and probation officer, Mark Steever. Mr. Steever listened to my plea for help and went the extra step to help me get it.

Thank you to the Phoenix Police Department and Phoenix Fire and Rescue Department for putting their lives on the line, minute by minute, to keep order and help everyone when we need it the most.

Thank you to all the people who allowed me to find sanctuary in their homes, when I was homeless and using, which keep me safe from harm. I am truly sorry for the pain and inconvenience I caused you all.

Thank you for the programs and people, who take part in Alcoholics Anonymous and Narcotics Anonymous, that allow time for people to share and facilities to gather together to give each other support.

Knowing

It was two weeks before Memorial weekend in 1986 and things were getting really bad in Bakersfield, California. I'd been staying with friends, and tearing their family apart. I was staying up all night and sleeping most of the day. My day consisted of making phone calls to get other people to support my cocaine habit. I would buy a quantity of cocaine with their cash and give them theirs, then use the extra to allow me some free stash.

I needed to get out of Bakersfield, so I called my brother JT who lived in Texas. I decided I needed a "geographical change". JT was a construction foreman for small remodel company, and had just landed a job with Texas A&M University. It was a big job, to install laboratory equipment, for the university's third chemistry building. He told me to pack my stuff and come on out.

A "geographical change" is what we call it in recovery, when we move from a bad location or situation, and expect things to change. It gave me hope, knowing I could start over in a different location, and possibly shake off my bad habits and bad relationships.

My older brother also lived in Houston. His name was LJ. He was awesome. I always looked up to him because he was a great role model, honest, athletic, hard-working and hand-some. I didn't stay in touch with him very much, because of the guilt I had for being such a screw-up. I called him up and told him what I was doing and asked if I could come spend the night with him and his new wife. He said no problem, and I packed up my stuff and hit the road.

All my belongings fit in my car, a 1976 yellow two-door Buick LeSabre. It was given to me by my Grandparents. I drove hard and was very tired from the long drive when I got there. We had a quick dinner, and I went to bed. The next day I got up, and we had some light conversation and I went to lay by the pool, at my brother's apartment complex.

It was a beautiful Texas day, and the weather was perfect for getting a great tan. There were several people at the pool. I made sure I selected a chair next to a gorgeous, well-built brunette named Lisa, who was a nurse. We started drinking some beers and got along great. She invited me to her place for dinner.

This was a typical example of how selfish and self-centered I was. I went to my brother and told him about the invitation and that I might not make it home that night. He had invited me into his home and I was blowing him off, after not seeing him for so many years. No wonder he didn't want anything to do with me. This was one of the many reasons.

Dinner was awesome. Lisa was a great cook. We had some wine and stripped-down and had passionate sex. She was so sexy and kind, a typical Texas beauty with class. I told her my birthday was the following weekend, and she told me she'd like to throw me a party. Actually, she already had a Memorial weekend party planned at her parent's house. She said they were quite well-to-do and had a really nice house and the party would be great. Some of her closest friends would be there and we could do an encore of tonight. I gladly accepted her offer and we had a great night's sleep.

It was Monday and I had to get up very early for my new job with my other brother, JT. It was about 6 am and I knocked on LJ's door. He answered the door a little agitated.

I told him thank you, grabbed my stuff and hit the road.

JT looked great. He was really in his element, being the boss. He was small in stature, well muscled and suntanned and looked 10 feet tall with his quick step, and smart wit. His crew was in the middle of a remodel down in the "gay district" of Montrose and Westheimer. We were going to do this job for the next week and then move to College Station. After a couple days, I was really starting to feel better, working with my shirt off and getting a great tan, but drinking heavily at night.

On Saturday, we packed up and moved to College Station. The lab furniture installation was very boring. JT would lay out the blueprints, and we would chalk in the measurements and plug the furniture in. I learned to "shim" cabinets. That is where you take a piece of small wood and push it under the cabinet to raise it to make it level. Boring!!! Thank God for the short work week. It was Memorial weekend.

I got up really early on Saturday morning and grabbed my cooler, iced my six-pack and headed to the pool. There was nothing like a beer buzz in the morning. I fell asleep and woke up about 2 PM with a great suntan. I felt great, took a shower, and put on my Gucci gold wristwatch and Varnier sunglasses. My red and white Varnier sunglasses were very cool and looked great with a suntanned face. The Gucci watch was the last thing I had bought with my American Express card that I didn't pay for, as my life had spiraled apart in Bakersfield. They were the last reminders of the good life I had as an engineer, before my credit went to shit because of my drug and alcohol addiction.

I got in my 1976 Buick LeSabre two-door, which was handed down to me from my grandmother. I called it the big banana car, because it was a yellow two-door machine with a black landau hardtop. I headed off to my birthday party. Lisa was matching it up with the party she had already planned for Memorial weekend at her parent's house, because they were out of town. I was a little hesitant because I had just met Lisa and I didn't want my birthday to interfere with her party and her friends. She assured me that it would be really cool, and her friends would love me. She reminded me that the house was awesome because her parents were very rich and had a beautiful home. She also assured me that she would be ready for a repeat engagement of the great sex we had, when I spent the night in her apartment. I was pumped up and excited.

The road between College Station and Houston was a typical Texas two-lane state route. One lane in each direction, up and down and twisting through the Texas forest terrain. With windows down and radio blaring, I put the pedal down and took off. The weather was beautiful, and after about 40 minutes of driving, a guy in a black Camaro or Trans Am came up behind me fast. I saw a radar detector in his windshield and sped up. I sped up to make better time, but also as a courtesy because it was almost impossible to pass on this road due to multiple hills and turns. There were caution lines, with glaring yellow paint, about every quarter mile and I didn't want to be rude and drive too slow. Plus, I welcomed the extra protection from the Texas Highway Patrol from his radar detector. The promise of the weekend bash at Lisa's felt closer than ever.

My radio was blaring; the south Texas wind was blowing in my windows when all of a sudden I heard a huge voice in my car that shook my whole body. It said; "PUT YOUR SEATBELT ON!!!!!!!!!!!!!!!!!!!!" Man, I freaked out!! I jerked around to see if someone was in my backseat. The voice was so loud and full. It echoed in my head and body. After the adrenaline rush, I calmed down and started thinking; "using my seatbelt makes sense, it is Memorial weekend and people could be driving drunk or too fast". I needed to put my seatbelt on, but it was broken! My Buick LeSabre was not equipped with shoulder belts, so I hooked to the passenger side.

About 20 minutes later, we came to the top of the hill. As we topped the hill, down about 300 yards was an intersection with a flashing yellow on our side and a flashing red on the road intersecting our state route. On both sides of the road there was barbed wire fencing that lined the forest on either side. On the far right side of the intersection was a barbed wire fence lining a cornfield, and a telephone light pole at the corner of the intersection. On the left-hand far corner was a small country store. On the left side of the intersection was a yellow Cadillac, and at the wheel was an old man with his two Doberman Pinschers; waiting their turn to cross the intersection after a stop at the country store.

When I came to the top of the hill, I saw the intersection. I slowed to 65 mph as we had been topping 75-85 mph, up and down around the Texas turns. When I was almost at the bottom of the hill, about 50 yards from the intersection, that SOB in the yellow Cadillac gunned his engine in attempt to cross the intersection before I reached it.

I slammed on my brakes, while veering to the right in an attempt to miss him, heading right for the telephone pole. Instead, I slammed directly into the yellow Cadillac. As I was being lifted from my seat, my head impacted the windshield as the collision began to eject me from the car, and I heard my neck crack. The very loose seatbelt that I had hooked over to the passenger side caught me. I jackknifed around the seatbelt and fell back into the bench seat as we slid to a stop.

I was seeing stars, just like the cartoon guys when they get knocked silly. The whole front end of my car was demolished and the front windshield was broken. My favorite sunglasses busted, and my last credit acquisition, my Gucci gold watch smashed to pieces. I started cussing as I stumbled out of my vehicle, ready to fight. The guy that was following me was right there to help me, as I stumbled out of my car. He may have even opened my door.

The store owner let me use his phone to call Lisa and

tell her what had happened. She said she would come get me. The cops came and had trouble getting the guy out of yellow Cadillac. He had passed out and the Dobermans were freaking out. They said he was drunk. I found out later he owned a local newspaper, and got out of the DUI charge.

Lisa came and picked me up. I was pretty shook up and starting to feel real pain. I wasn't much fun at Lisa's party. She said I was in shock. I called my brother to arrange for him to pick me up on Sunday to take me back to College Station. I went to bed before the party was over. Lisa came to bed after midnight, and we made slow passionate love, and I dozed off to sleep.

I woke up to Lisa's soft voice about 11 AM, with the smell of a great Texas country breakfast in the air. She asked if I was okay and told me breakfast was ready. I started to get up and couldn't move. I was really messed up. Lisa had to help me get out of the bed. She told me she had a feeling the night before, when she saw my vehicle and heard about "the Voice" and the loose seatbelt, that I would probably be in bad shape in a day or two, and she was right.

My brother picked me up about 2 PM and we headed to an Emergency Care clinic to get me fixed up. One good thing; I had a fresh script of Vicodin, Flexeril and Soma. Diagnosis: soft tissue injuries from my neck down my spine to my rear, but I was alive!...........and if it not been for "the Voice" in my car yelling to put my seatbelt on, I probably would've been dead or paralyzed after ejecting through my windshield.

There's no doubt in my mind that this was a Miracle, an Angelic intervention to keep me from dying. I was alive and **knowing** there had to be a reason for me living.

Beginning

I was born the second/third son; twin sons of Sharon Mosby and Jerry Mosby on May 20, 1962. My twin's name was Glen Shannon. My older brother LJ, was one year older and my younger brother JT, was one year younger.

My father was born in Granite City, Illinois. He and his older brother and my Granddad and Granny Ercie, moved to southern Missouri, when he was very young. Granny opened a small store in Springfield, Missouri which served the local area.

My father was small in stature and excelled in sports, especially individual sporting competitions. He was a Golden Gloves boxing champion and was a perfect example of "little man's complex" or "Napoleon complex". He was also a perfect example of what can happen to people when they have painful voids and losses and guilt in their lives. When things went wrong, he did many different things to medicate or try to forget, to get a quick thrill to replace his feelings.

He met my Mom and she fell in love with his charisma and personality. He was a natural born salesman, a hereditary trait. No one really approved of their relationship for many reasons, where he was from, no college, etc. Jerry always had great opportunities due to his personality and "hard at it" short-term work ethic, but if it didn't move fast enough or upward quick enough, he was out and on to other things.

We loved Mom and Dad. Mom was so loving and supportive. Dad was full of fun most of the time, when I remember his brief interludes (I found out later he was not around all the time).

My mother was born in Cassville, Missouri; a very small rural town. She was the oldest of four siblings; all-female. Her mother and father built a respected insurance agency, which allowed all the daughters to be involved in all aspects of life, growing up at home and away at college. They had a very nice home, nice clothes, participated in extra-curricular activities and went to good colleges. Her mother and father were both God-fearing and very active in church. Granddad was an avid fisherman and loved taking my brothers and I fishing for goggle eye and sun perch, with an occasional brown bass in the mix. The best part of the fishing was catching the bait in the fast flowing Missouri streams. We would take a heavy wire grate-like net and place it into the rocks. Granddad turned over rocks upstream, which stirred up an amazing creature called hellgrammites. They came loose in the fast flowing streams and got caught in the grate. They were like centipedes with pincher type appendages coming from their heads and their back was like the shell of a lobster. They were great bait—the fish loved them. We always came back with lots of fish to eat.

I always looked forward to meeting Granddad in church for second service, as he was an usher and attended both services. We would dress up and run to meet him. He always commented how he loved my singing. I always sat by him so he could hear me sing.

Nana was awesome too; always a good planner director and organizer, and she loved to see us arrive at her house on weekend visits. She would always go with Mom, Granddad and us boys, when we would visit in the summer to pick strawberries. She would fix them up with my mom, and get the shortcake and strawberries ready for strawberry short-cake. She also made the best homemade donuts. I remember being too excited to sleep the night before, thinking about how they would smell cooking the next morning when we got up.

My mom was awesome. My grandparents raised her and her sisters with a good work ethic and faith that stands the test of time. Values this great country was built on. They all turned out great, except one of their lives was cut short by a drunk driver.

My mom was great student, beautiful, and she loved to sing and dance and play piano, and she had a great figure. She was a tri-Delta sorority sister and graduated with a teaching degree. All of these great traits attracted my father; who stole her heart and broke it, but together they made four beautiful Sons. My mom gave birth to my older brother, LJ. Then about fifteen months later; twins, Shannon and I. Fifteen months later, JT was born.

At nine months old; my twin brother Shannon got sick with pneumonia, and died. It was a huge tragedy. My dad blamed our family doctor; a good friend of my grandparents. Supposedly Shannon was doing better, so the doctor said it was okay to let him go home. As the story goes, I heard the nuns thought just the opposite. But when he got home, Shannon got worse and by the time he returned to the hospital, he died. I never thought this could have affected me because I was so young. I found out later, this was my first **loss/void.** It was hard for everybody and affected everyone's relationship, my mom, my dad, grandparents and their friends.

TheFreeDictionary.com and Merriam-Webster.com define void as: An empty space; useless, feeling of want; being without something; a feeling of emptiness, loneliness or loss. They define loss as: harm resulting from separation; condition of being deprived or bereaved of something or someone; uncertain of what to do; the harm resulting from separation.

Dad's "little man's complex" escalated with drinking, gambling, stealing, falsifying identities, check forgery, auto theft, etc. He wasn't around much and when he was, it seemed like discipline time for me. He usually entered the scene with a burst of fun, hugs, "I love you's" and discipline. He was extra hard on me, belt instead of hands for spanking, four times instead of one or two. I now believe it was the pain of Shannon's death reflected on me; but still I loved and worshiped him. Later, as I grew older, we became great friends.

Mom was a schoolteacher. She got home about an hour after we did from school, so we usually used that time to start homework. Fun could start from then on. Mom helped us develop this study habit which would help me and my brothers get great grades in high school and college, when it really mattered.

By the time I was in second grade, my dad wasn't around much. My mom was teaching school and providing for us all on her own. Dad hadn't been around for many weeks and my mom would always say he's working.

One day, when she got home after school, she gathered us all together and told us she had something to tell us. I was in the fourth grade, and I remember this like it was yesterday. She told us that my dad would not be coming home and they were going to get a divorce. I cried my eyes out for what seemed like hours. I had never cried that hard before. This was my second **void/loss.** The heartbreak, loneliness and emptiness I felt was so terrible.

I noticed at different times, men would come to the door and ask for Jerry (Dad). My mom would step out and talk to them. A short time later, Mom came home from school and said she had to talk to us again. This time, she told us that Dad had gotten himself in trouble. She said that there was an article in the paper and that people might start saying something to us. She said we didn't need to respond to them, but we could tell them we don't know anything about it.

Several days later, one of my Cub Scout friends started talking about it in school, calling my dad a jailbird and a thief. It really upset me and I told Mom that day after school. The next day, I punched him out. The combinations that Dad had taught us, with our brief Golden Gloves boxing lessons, worked out better than they did in a real match. I bloodied his nose and got in trouble. We moved to a different school district that summer. I was becoming very angry. I was turning my feelings of abandonment, from my father leaving, into anger.

My mom provided for my two brothers and I like a saint. We all played on basketball, baseball and football teams. She went to 3+ ballgames per week and worked full-time, all through our junior high and high school years. She also went to night school to get her Master's degree to make more pay. She also worked Friday and Saturday nights at the local newspaper to make more money to take care of her boys. We went to church every Sunday and never lacked for anything. We always had clean clothes and plenty to eat and Mom never complained. She had turned her loss/void into caring for us—true love.

We were all very smart, athletic and attractive. The new neighborhood had some very affluent families. Junior high began my experimentation with sexual encounters and marijuana. In the eighth grade, one day after basketball practice, two other players, one bad boy with long hair and a rich kid's son and a sexy cheerleader decided to go to "the trees" to smoke. "The trees" was a 20'tall x 10'wide barrier that grew around the two-acre practice field for football and gym classes. I overheard them and asked if I could come along. There was about 20 minutes till my mother would be there to pick us up after practice. We got into the tree line, away from

view and the long hair pulled out a fat, strange shaped cigarette and said it was cool, a joint; Mary Jane. I smoked and
coughed. They chastised me and told me to hold it in for long
as possible. I tried again and held it in. I know some people
say you don't get high the first time, but I did. By the time
my mom got there I felt like my woolen winter coat reeked
of it. I was paranoid Mom could smell it. I was very high.
She gave me a silly look. I was giddy and was making my
little brother JT laugh, too. This was my first substitution or
attempt to fill "the void" that had been developing in my life.

I started taking guitar lessons in the fifth grade. I was
getting pretty good with an acoustic sound like Crosby, Stills
and Nash, John Denver, and Glen Campbell fashion with a
voice like an angel. I was in choir at school and competing
in many singing competitions. In the eighth and ninth grade,
I was a finalist on a local TV channel talent search com-
petition. I won second place the first time (due to my song
choice being wrong, that was my own and no one knew me), a
small-town guy won first place because everyone in his town
voted for him. Supposedly everybody else voted for me. The
second time, I won by a landslide, singing and playing guitar
to "Space Cowboy".

I was a quarterback in junior high school. We filtered
into senior high, and I was up against the rival competing
quarterback from another junior high school. We started practice two weeks before high school. The first week was just
drills and the second week, with pads. Then the first day of
school arrived. It was awesome and an exciting promise of
conquering the school, a great sports career and practice after
school.

We started out with typical warm-up and stretching cal-
isthenics and then we broke up into groups to start drills.
My group was doing a practice drill, called "Oklahoma" or
"Hamburger" because you got smashed in the drill. Here's
how it worked: there were two practice dummies laid on the

ground 5 yards apart then two linemen set across from each other, facing each other. There was also a running back and linebacker. The offensive lineman and running back decided which way the lineman would block so the running back would run through the hole. The defensive lineman would practice throwing the block and tackling the running back and the linebacker would charge through the hole and tackle the running back practicing form and strength. I was the linebacker.

The running back called "hut" and the offensive lineman exploded off the line and attempted to open the hole, so the running back could run through. I rushed forward, and hit the running back and picked him up, practicing good form, and drove him backwards. The speed and forward momentum of my tackle was stopped in its tracks, as the two linemen joined the fun and piled on top. My right leg was behind me as their weight pushed me straight down, and my right football cleat stuck in the ground. My right foot didn't move, as it was stuck as I fell. The scene changed into slow-motion as I fell backwards and down and my right femur bone snapped in half. It sounded like a huge tree limb breaking off in the forest in winter with the weight of the heavy snow. With the bone being in compression as it broke, it slid side by side, ripping the muscle from the side of bone which then sent a bloodcurdling scream from my lungs from a deep pitch to a high pitch. It sent electrifying pains shooting from the top of my spine to the bottom of my body. My leg was flapping to the right side of my body, with my foot and ankle behind my neck and my knee at a right angle to my body.

I went into shock, as pain surged throughout my body. My vision decreased to a small space with fuzz around the peripheral vision. My football coach was a heavyset Christian man named Coach Bayless. He never cursed and frowned on it greatly. I knew I was screwed when he yelled "Oh my God", and ran like a sprinter to the gym to get help.

Now keep in mind, my femur is broken, and my leg is to the right side of my body. My knee is bent and my foot is behind my neck like an unnatural hurdler stretch. The varsity coach who had not seen the accident came up from the main field to help. With my pain and agony and writhing around my leg had straightened out little bit, but was still very crooked. As I was laying there moaning, he started moving my leg and said, "I don't think it's broken". He attempted to pull my foot out from behind my head and sent me through another burst of pain as my muscles ripped further from the bone. He shouted several obscenities and told everyone to get back. My leg was flopping back and forth now with my writhing around so he put a football helmet under it to keep it from hitting the ground.

The ambulance came driving onto the practice field. The paramedics diagnosed the situation and advised me it was going to hurt. They took two boards (mobile traction unit) under my legs, one on each side and snapped them together. The varsity coach held my hand as they pulled my foot forward and placed my leg in temporary traction. I almost broke my coach's hand. I had to listen to the paramedics talk about my damn broken leg all the way to the hospital. I was really pissed off and football was out the door. **Another void/loss.**

The emphasis put on sports, with all the practice and being good at it, was such a part of my life, I was seized with a pain I couldn't define. I had questions and no adequate answers. Why is this happening? I had so much riding on my plans of playing football and other sports. What was I going to do now? Without intervention from other positive sources, I would be drawn away from God and fill my void with other things (quick fixes) of this world.

I lay on a gurney in the hallway for over an hour waiting to go to surgery. People were walking by and gawking at me. I was so glad when my mom got there to hold my hand in the hallway.

We found that we had a choice. They could cut an 18 inch hole up and down my thigh and put a rod in my leg. I would be walking and back-to-school within 30 days. The second choice was, they could drill a pin in my knee, and put a horseshoe splint on it with a rope over pulleys and a weight attached. With this option, I would stay in the hospital for one and a half months and have a walking body cast for two to three months. This second choice would leave no scar.

In surgery, they shot my knee area with injections to deaden it. This was in preparation to drill a hole into my front shinbone to attach a pin to hang the weights on. This would allow them to pull my bone apart so it could rest together to start mending. The doctor said nothing and pulled out a drill that looked like one you see, used to drill a hole in a board and attached a quarter inch stainless steel pin to it. He hit the trigger several times. The bloodcurdling high-pitched drill sound sent chills down my body and the orderly said "hold my hand, it is going to hurt".

The doctor started drilling into my skin, and I could feel blood spurting. When it hit the bone I almost passed out. The pin popped out the other side, and the doctor moved it in and out (it had to be loose so it could be removed later). They took boards and put a harness under my leg with a halo around my leg, at the thigh and hip area, to hold onto. Then they attached a cord to a stainless steel horseshoe which was connected to the pin and threaded it over the pulleys and attached the weights to it, and pulled out my leg into traction.

One week later, the doctor came in and said everything was fine, but he had to make sure the pin stayed mobile so it could be removed in a month or so. It was very sore where it came out of the skin. It had very painful blood clots in the shape of donuts around its exit of the skin. He took hold of the horseshoe that was attached to the cord which was attached to the weights for traction, and started wrenching it forward and backwards ripping the blood clots open and sending pain up and down my spine. He did this every three or four days until there was no pain at all. They gradually reduced the weight and my leg angle proceeded to almost be horizontal. This took about a month. One day, they came and knocked me out and I woke up with a walking body cast; and they sent me home.

I missed the whole first three months of school. I had a great private tutor who did a good job keeping me up with my classes. I started planning then how to graduate early and get out. I had missed the first three months of entering my new school. I had worked so hard at my goals of playing football and had lost that opportunity. I was mad and very disappointed.

Life went on, and I got my cast off. I made the track team in the spring, with no spectacular results. The next year, I played a second string position on the football team. I was told I probably wouldn't play football again. I only tried out for football to prove I could play again. I quit team sports after that.

I was really good at playing guitar and singing. I performed at several talent contests around town in bars and at the Grand Old Opry in town. I answered an ad in our local newspaper, placed by a talent scout from Nashville, Tennessee. My mom and I met the scout from Fuse Productions at a local motel. He said he really liked my sound, the way I looked and thought I would be marketable. He wanted to cut a master record and see how it went over. My mom and I talked about it and decided that I would get my engineering degree first. I could wait and cut a master record after I graduated. You are only young once. I was really upset at this decision. Another void.

College-bound

It was 1978, the summer before my junior year and my plan to graduate early from high school was going as planned. We needed an extra car, as my older brother and I were both driving and JT would be driving next summer.

My uncle Freddie (dad's only brother) was a mechanical engineer working and living in Huntsville, Alabama. He had an old 1966 Chrysler Imperial four door tank he would give to us if we came down and got it. So my mom and my two brothers planned a road trip and headed to Alabama.

I was always good at mathematics and science, and the experience with my broken leg and traction had fascinated me about physics and engineering. Uncle Freddie was in the nuclear engineering business. I always loved talking with him and hearing stories of when he worked for Rocketdyne, where he helped design engines that fueled the NASA rockets.

When I was in the hospital for six weeks and at home for over a month, I had a lot of time to think. I planned to become an engineer and scheduled my algebra and geometry class the same year, so I could take math analysis my junior year and graduate early at mid term. I would be out of high school and onto real life, leaving sports and disappointments behind.

I had also gotten quite good at making good grades while smoking marijuana daily. We also experimented with LSD on weekends, as we used it to get close to God. We used marijuana and LSD to elevate our religious experience. We also experimented with cocaine, pills and PCP and lots of alcohol to medicate our voids and losses.

The summer before my senior year in 1979, I met a gorgeous 18-year-old that had just graduated from high school in Nebraska that summer. She moved to Springfield, with her family, when her dad had bought a bar.

I was playing my guitar, singing and getting high at our local hangout, "Peckers Beach". It was our local make-out and party spot on the James River. She was on a date with some guy and made him pull over and get out, so they could come and hear me play guitar and sing. She gave me her number and I called her the next week and we got together. She was built like Dorothy Stratton (my favorite Playboy bunny, who had been shot dead by her jealous husband). She was ready, and I filled my void with sex; and then we got pregnant.

In the spring of 1980, I went to my first semester at the University of Missouri-Rolla, as a nuclear engineering student. I still had long hair and wouldn't cut it just to prove a point that "longhairs" could get good grades. I got straight A's and then cut my hair. I came home to Springfield for the summer, and in August my beautiful twin boys were born.

I went back to school in the fall and continued to get great grades, excelling in class. We got married in November. She and the boys moved up to Rolla that spring, and we stayed in married student housing and began looking for little house. I started planning interviews to get a summer job in the nuclear engineering industry, then the "3 Mile Island nuclear event" occurred, and there were no summer jobs.

I found out that Petroleum Engineers were the top paid engineers coming out of school and had great summer jobs while in college. I landed a good summer job with Amoco in Corpus Christi Texas, as a roustabout engineering trainee. We loaded up the twins in the Galaxy 500, and headed to the beach.

On our way to Corpus Christi we broke down just outside Dallas. My mom brought us our family station wagon so we could make it through the summer. We got to Corpus and found a really cool third floor condo, right on the water. I carpooled with three other engineers to a location about 40 minutes from downtown Corpus. It was a great job and the weather was awesome.

There were two women that lived in the complex together. They were both on welfare and they were gossipy, nosy and big partiers. They hung out with one of the maintenance men. He was also a big loser. We started partying with them on weekends, and my wife hung around them during the week.

One weekend, when we returned from the beach, one of these women told me that my wife had slept with the maintenance man. I went to their apartment and confronted my wife as this guy stood by. He started running his mouth to me. I was ready to unload on him, when my wife stood up and started defending him. I was shocked and enraged and turned around and told her to shut her mouth. I slapped her with an open hand and she went down.

The two women pushed me out of their apartment and ran to my apartment and took the twins out of their cribs and back to their place. The next morning I had to drive in the carpool, so I left very early. When I came home, the apartment was completely packed and I was told her dad was coming to get her and take her and the twins back to Missouri. The next night I came home from work, and they were gone. Another **void/loss. My parent's divorce had hurt me deeply. I vowed that I never wanted to get a divorce. The emptiness, regret and sense of failure I felt, with my children being taken away, quickly turned to resentment which filled the void.**

I still had three weeks of work left. I finished the job and loaded up my stuff and headed back to Missouri by myself.

I stopped at the same hotel in Richardson, Texas that we had stayed in when our car broke down. I met a beautiful 5'2" blonde haired waitress in the bar and invited her to my room later. She came up about 10 PM and we had awesome sex for hours. It filled my void, and I used that technique as often as possible to make me feel good for many years to come.

I continued to do very well in college. My mom had taught us great study habits, so it made studying very easy. I interviewed and got another great summer job this time in sunny Bakersfield, California.

On my way out to Bakersfield, I spent the night in Flagstaff, Arizona. I went out and had a nice dinner, a few drinks and then went to a nightclub. I met some people who invited me to their house for an after-hours party. On my way back to the hotel I was kind of lost. It was about 2:30 in the morning and a policeman pulled me over, I had been speeding 5 miles over the speed limit. I could see my hotel from where he pulled me over. I got a DUI.

I finished my summer job and got my court date postponed until my Christmas break. My mom helped me out again. On my winter break, we drove to Arizona, went to court, paid my fines and drove back to Missouri. We negotiated a SIS (suspended imposition of sentence), which would be reduced to misdemeanor, if I passed my probation period.

Graduation

I went back to school and lived off campus in a small dormitory apartment. We began divorce proceedings and she put me through hell with the visitation guidelines, so I had to spend a little money getting everything written down. My parent's divorce had really hurt me and I wanted to stay married. This divorce really upset me. Another **void/loss**. My distrust of women fueled my personal relationships for years to come.

I graduated Cum Laude with Honors, and got a great job with Chevron, USA in Bakersfield. I loved the desert. I was employed as a production engineer in the Taft, California production office. I didn't like the office part much, but loved being in the field.

I started partying a lot and falling asleep at work, because of staying up too late. Then, I got fired. All that school, and fired from my dream job. Another **void/loss.** Then, the medicating of my pain skyrocketed. I call it the "f—- it" attitude. Just blow off everything and have a good time. I would worry about the consequences later.

I had met some cool and wild "coke people" and had partied on occasion with my next-door neighbor. I had given him coke but never saw him do any. He always had a reason for not doing it at that moment and said he would do it later. One day, he came over and told me to come to his apartment. He told me he had some good coke and asked me if I wanted him to "fix" me. I didn't know what he meant and then he showed me the needle.

I was repulsed at first, but my other buddy was there and he told me it would be cool because they had fresh needles and alcohol, so I tried it—what a rush! I was used to the high from smoking cocaine; "freebasing", but the mainline experience got me hooked even more. Soon, I sold all my stuff and got evicted from my apartment and moved in with some friends.

I still seemed to be able to maintain paying one of my credit cards. It had a high limit and I used it to pay some of my expenses. I still knew enough people that had jobs and liked to party; I could get their money up front and buy some dope. I would give them theirs, make a little money and have some free stash. I would go out at night to party, meet a hot chick and stay with her for a while.

I had met a real sexy, skinny, beautiful drug dealer. She had her own place, she paid her own way and we had great sex. One morning, I got up early and the Mustang I had been renting was out of gas. I was dressed really nice and I walked around the corner to a Circle K to get some gasoline. I had a container that wasn't an authorized container, and didn't know that was a law. The guy at the counter was very aggressive about denying me the ability to buy gas. We had words, and the next thing I knew the police were there. I should've kept my mouth shut, but when I pleaded my case, the cop decided to search me. I had a deering (paraphernalia used to grind drugs into a powder) in my pocket, and the cop found it. I started screaming that he had planted it and stuck to that story. They took me to the police station and later let me go, but kept my drugs. It was another close call.

My drug use was continuing to get worse. I was at a party, at a friend of a friend's house, and I went to the bathroom to get high. I had a little trick that I used to mix my cocaine and water for mainlining. I used my contact lens case for a spoon. No one would ever suspect what it was for. I fixed my hit and shot up. I remember my legs getting wobbly as I was hiding my syringe inside my hidden jacket pocket; where I had already hidden my stash and my lens case. I had been in the bathroom a long time. People were banging on the door telling me to let them in. I opened the door and was stumbling around delirious. Someone said they were calling the police and a girlfriend of mine, ushered me out the door to try and protect me. The police caught up with me in the parking lot, as I was getting in her car and arrested me for being under the influence.

They searched me really well, but didn't find my syringe or stash. I was handcuffed with my hands behind me, but was able to stash my syringe under the front seat of the patrol car, by pushing it with my feet. We got to the station, then the officer un-handcuffed me and told me to spread eagle and put my hands on the counter. The officer re-searched me and pulled my handkerchief out of my rear pocket, making a joke about carrying "boogers" around in my pocket.

There were a bunch of prisoners in a holding cell, about 5 feet behind me and several police officers at the other end of the corridor. The officer found the hidden pocket on one side of my jacket, which was now empty and I knew it would be seconds before he found my eightball (slang for an eighth of an ounce of cocaine). My adrenaline was flowing and I was pissed off about the handkerchief comment. I knew I had to act fast. I grabbed the edge of the counter and crow hopped onto my right foot and lifted my left leg and kicked the cop in the back of the head. His head hit the counter and he went down. I grabbed the eight ball and bit it open, swallowed it and headed for the cellblock. The inmates were applauding and screaming like crazy. The cop I had kicked in the head, and three of his buddies, tackled me and tried to get me to spit out the coke. One of the cops put his hand down my throat almost to his elbow, but I had swallowed it. They roughed me up a little bit, re-handcuffed me, and threw me in a private cell.

It wasn't long before I started getting in distress. My heart rate was really racing and they knew they had to get me to the hospital, fast. I knew from chemistry that a lot of the cocaine would get tied up by my body acid in my stomach, but if too much got into my system, I was a goner. After they got me to the hospital, they tried to get me to drink a chemical to make me throw up. I refused because I didn't want them to have any evidence. After a little while, a doctor came in and told me to look at the heart monitor. He convinced me that I would die if I didn't throw up quick, so I drank it.

I was handcuffed to the gurney and overheard the policemen talking. They said the officer guarding me, was a karate cop. They thought that I knew karate because I had kicked my arresting officer in the head, like a ninja.

It took a long time to throw up. I hadn't eaten much for a couple of days so I knew there wasn't anything else in my stomach. The officer guarding me started flirting with a good looking nurse and wasn't paying attention. When he wasn't looking, I threw up. Out came the rest of the baggy, which I hid under the bed. The rest of my vomit was clear and milky white. I dumped it on the floor, so there was no more evidence.

My felony possession charge was dismissed. I pled guilty

to a misdemeanor obstruction of justice charge, for destroying evidence. I got lucky twice. I didn't do any jail time and I was alive.

I had to get out of there. I called my little brother JT and told him what was going on. He told me to come to Texas and work for him. I packed my whole life in my 1976 Buick LeSabre, hit the road and made it to Houston. Two weeks later, on Memorial weekend of 1986, I had my "Voice experience" telling me to put my seatbelt on, which saved my life.

Geographical

After my car accident, I was in bed for almost a month and in heavy therapy for two months. My little brother, JT was awesome. He was still doing the job in College Station and would come home from work twice a day to take me to therapy. I was really messed up. I had therapy two times a day for one month, and then once a day for the next month. I had retained an attorney for my personal injury lawsuit who arranged for the chiropractor to be paid upon settlement. He also had a buddy, who owned a small car lot and sold me a 1979 Dodge Magnum two-door. He waited for payment until we settled my lawsuit.

I had outstayed my welcome with JT and our roommate. I got a little money from the accident lawsuit, settled up with JT and hit the road to Fort Lauderdale, Florida. I wanted to get a job on the "Love Boat". I had waited tables through college and thought it would be great, doing a service job on a cruise ship. I got to Fort Lauderdale and started trying to look up numbers for interviews to get a job on a cruise line. I was shocked to find out they didn't hire at Fort Lauderdale. They hired mainly out of New York and the "Love Boat" didn't exist. They didn't hire many Americans, mostly low-paid wage people from indigent countries. I found a job waiting tables at a local Steak n' Ale and found a room for rent in the newspaper. I now lived in sunny Florida, another new start.

I couldn't seem to get ahead. I went out on a gambling cruise ship and got pick-pocketed and lost my wallet. The transmission in my new car when out. I took it to a transmission place and the owner took my nice diamond ring as collateral to start the work. I had to work double shifts, just to pay for my taxi to and from work and have a little extra cash. I contacted my cousin, who was an engineer in Vero Beach, Florida. He was one of the coolest guys I knew. He loaned me the money to get my car out of hock and I've never paid him back (I've tried for years to find him to thank him and repay him).

The big nightlife in Fort Lauderdale was "bartender and waitress" clubs. They opened at 1 AM in the morning and stayed open until noon the next day. I met a guy there that said he needed a roommate, so I moved in with him. I got a new job at the exclusive Boca Raton Hotel and Club. I was in the room service department and started making pretty steady money.

One morning, after leaving a B&W club; I rear-ended a lady on her way to work. I was driving wasted with a hot chick and heading to my apartment. My car would not go in reverse so I had to have it towed to my apartment. I had exchanged insurance information with the lady and we took off before the cops arrived. I barely avoided a DUI. I was out of money, my car was broken, and I hated Florida.

I bought a ticket to my hometown, Springfield, Missouri and left my stereo system, turntable, speakers and all my vinyl records at my apartment. I packed my clothes in a suitcase, put on my gray tuxedo and tails, left my car in the parking lot and boarded a Greyhound bus for Springfield.

It was the spring of 1987, and my awesome mother allowed me to move in with her until I got back on my feet. I got a job at a local restaurant waiting tables and started saving for a car. It was easy in Springfield to make friends and to get rides from people at work. My customers loved me, and I met lots of new people. I was very selfish and self-centered, and only thought about myself. All my relationships were centered in what people could do for me. I met a couple in the restaurant, who offered me a job teaching dance lessons. They owned the dance studio and taught me how to ballroom dance and to teach lessons. I didn't like how they tried to take advantage of older women, by selling them high priced dance lesson packages as they got more advanced. One afternoon I overheard one of the managers telling the teacher, to ask the student to take a second mortgage out on her house, to pay for the $15,000 dance lesson package. It rubbed me the wrong way, so I picked up my jacket and walked out. Another customer at the restaurant, told me I would be good at selling cars, so I switched jobs to selling new cars at Friendly Ford, a family owned car dealership.

At the restaurant, I had also met a beautiful woman and her husband, and for the first time fell in love with someone. I really liked her husband and children. They treated me like family. I didn't mean to hurt them, but I did. They were very affluent and had a great reputation in town. I knew it was getting out of control. I was such an asshole. I felt so guilty. He even cosigned for a car for me and I rented an apartment from him and his partner. The relationship was really messed up. I wasn't seeing anyone else, and I started using drugs again.

Many nights, she would call me between 10:30 and 11 PM, when her husband was in the shower, getting ready for bed. I thought he had gotten pretty suspicious lately. He bugged their telephone and heard a recording of her call to me, after he got out of shower. He called me and told me, "If you don't get the f—- out my apartment, I will come in the middle of the night and stick a needle in your neck". He was a doctor and I believed him. My drug use was also spurring bouts of paranoia, so I couldn't sleep there anymore.

Several months before, I had gotten pulled over for drunk

driving. Back then, the first offense could be reduced to a misdemeanor with probation. I also paid a fine and filed an SR 22 filing for high-risk auto insurance. I had my final hearing and wrote my $154 check to the high risk insurance company in Farmington, Missouri. I packed up all my stuff in my 1986 Pontiac T 1000, and headed back to Bakersfield to try and get back in the oil business.

First death — HEAVEN

When I got back to Bakersfield, I stayed with the old friends and family I had lived with before. The oil business still wasn't hiring engineers, so I got a job selling Mercedes –Benz cars. This started going well, but after 6 months, I got fired for borrowing cars and missing work. I was getting really high with quality drugs bought with my good income from the car sales. I got a part-time job doing singing telegrams and strip o' grams for daily cash money. By chance, I ran into an old neighbor of mine from 1983, who was with her daughter. I started dating her daughter and would spend the night at their apartment sometimes and with my other family, when I needed a break.

My girlfriend and her mother were pretty straight. They drank, but no drugs. It was almost Christmas and I just scored a quarter ounce of almost pure cocaine. I didn't usually snort my cocaine. I would freebase it and smoke it.

I believe that one of God's special methods of helping a drug addict want to quit using drugs, is the onset of extreme paranoia with drug use. In the beginning of the onset of para-noia, while the user is still halfway rational, it is designed to allow people to be embarrassed enough by their actions when around others, to decide to quit using. If that didn't work, then the paranoia would get so bad, that it wouldn't be any fun to get high anymore.

I had been trying to sneak a "good hit" for hours by going

to the bathroom to get high and going out to my car and bending over to hide behind the seat to take a hit, and it was driving me crazy. I had tried to go to sleep with my girlfriend and I just laid there for what seemed like hours. I finally got up and tried to watch TV while trying to sneak a good hit. I kept watching the hallway trying to see if her or her mom were coming out of the bedroom. It kept ruining my hit, from the paranoia of getting caught. It was Christmas Eve, and finally morning came.

I got in the shower and waited until about eight o'clock and called an engineering buddy of mine, who was single and liked to party. To my surprise, he was home alone and accepted my invitation to get high, on Christmas Day. Christmas day, how sick was that. I packed up my paraphernalia and hid my dope in my underwear. I told my girlfriend and her mother good morning and Merry Christmas and hit the road. I carefully drove over to my friend's house.

He opened the door in his bathrobe, welcomed me in and called "first hit", as was the custom to decide who would get the first chance to hit the pipe. He had a beautiful two-story split-level condo. The garage was in the back of the house, accessed by an alley parking spot. The front of the house had vaulted ceilings in the living room area and had a stairwell leading up the back wall, to the top floor with multiple bedrooms lining the railing, overlooking the living room.

As I entered the house through the back door into the kitchen and dining area, he asked me if I wanted something to drink. I said that a beer would be perfect. We went into the living room, and as usual, his bachelor pad was clean and neat. He had two black leather couches and a big glass table, a big-screen TV and sparse Christmas decorations.

I sat down and took out the container with my pipe, some cotton balls and a small half pint of Bacardi 151 rum. He got a shot glass to put the rum in and I pulled a cotton ball apart and wrapped it around a metal stick, which created a torch to light the pipe. We used 151, because unlike alcohol, it burns clean and didn't choke us. He took the first hit and sat back, held his breath and blew out the smoke. He got an awesome first hit. I already had prepared a big batch of freebase, chunks of pure cocaine ready to smoke. I put the rest of my powder on the table (about an eighth of an ounce) in a plastic baggie and told him to get ready to blow out the torch when I was done taking my hit.

Part of paranoia, when starting to get high, is the onslaught of shadowy figures. I believe it is the manifestation of Angels, which could be good or bad, but I tend to believe evil, waiting to take their final form in the act of collecting the sinning soul. I believe that due to my inability to take a good hit, through my multiple attempts in the last 24 hours, I had saturated my pipe with unused cocaine. This made sense, and I could tell it was true, because of the rush my buddy got on his first hit.

I was so relieved, with the sense of security knowing I had come to a place, which was safe to get high in. I slowly pushed all my breath out, lit the torch, dropped in the rock and started inhaling slowly and deeply. As I was nearing the end of my inhalation, I started getting off. At the exit door, leading to the back of the house through the kitchen, I started noticing shadowy figures. Then along the stairway, across the balcony at the top floor of the stairs were numerous black shadowy figures, as real and bold as I'd ever seen before. As I tried to cry out and point them out to my buddy, I spoke but nothing came out and everything went black.

I felt a very sudden acceleration of my body upward and the noise and feeling of strong wind. The acceleration was upward, changing angles and racing upward, and all of a sudden Whoosh. Almost immediately, my senses became alive and I felt as though I was floating upward. All around me was a light blue and white color with the sounds of thousands of voices singing and changing octaves "Aah, Aah, Aah, Aah, Aah, Aah, Aah, Aah". But I noticed in my field of vision, were thousands upon thousands upon thousands of angelic, white shadowy figures lining up in rows upon rows all around me like a coliseum row upon row upon row. I continued to ascend upward slowly floating with the voices singing and changing octaves "Aah, Aah, Aah, Aah, Aah, Aah". It was such beautiful singing. I felt so comfortable and happy. In the Tao religion, they believe that in heaven, there are many layers and levels. That may have been what I was seeing. I do believe I was being judged.

All of a sudden, there was blackness and I felt like I was being accelerated again, downward. Very quickly, straight down, and I heard thousands of screaming deep, guttural voices shouting in some eastern Mediterranean or Arabic language. I had the feeling of things grabbing me and trying to pull me down. It reminded me of the movie "Ghost", when the demons came after people and tried to pull them down to hell.

I woke up coughing and gasping for air with my arms, swinging wildly and my heart racing. My buddy was standing there freaking out with blood all over his face and robe, screaming at me to stop and get out.

I looked around and there was blood all over the walls and his curtains were torn up on one of his beautiful etched living room windows, and the window was cracked. His living room glass table was shattered. I was gasping and still catching my breath, and I asked him what happened. He told me, when I took my hit I started passing out and I dropped the pipe and fell through the table and broke it as I passed out. He said he had checked me and I had quit breathing. I had cut my hand and arm from falling through and breaking the glass table. That is where the blood came from. I called him a liar. He yelled at me, "You passed out and quit breathing, Mother F—-er and busted my table. I gave you mouth-to-mouth and saved your life. I beat on your chest and you still weren't breathing. Again, I gave you mouth-to-mouth. When you started breathing, you jumped up and started going crazy and busted my window and bled all over the place".

I start apologizing, and he just started telling me to get out. I asked for my quarter ounce bag of dope and he said he flushed it. I called him a liar and he said he was going to call the cops on me if I didn't leave. My heart was racing and I wrapped my bandanna around my cut and stumbled out the back door.

I bled all over my car. I could hardly drive. I was so shook up and my heart was still racing. Where can I go? I knew I would be safe at the family's house I used to stay with. I made it there, and the wife opened the door and gasped as she asked me what had happened. I shook and cried for hours. My heart still was out of rhythm for hours. I was very scared. I had seen Heaven, and had been grabbed by my heels by Hell. I believe I was judged and given a second chance.

Extradition

I stayed in bed for about three days before my body felt halfway normal and my fear subsided. I needed to get my own place. So, I started looking in the newspaper and found a room for rent. It was a nice place, with a swimming pool and two lady roommates. One owned it, and the other renter was her friend.

I got a job waiting tables. I usually slept in late, worked a double shift and got home late. On my days off, I would lay by the pool and go out at night and sometimes not come home, because I got lucky. I was on my second month of rent when I had met a lady I started seeing regularly. It was three days before rent was due and I hadn't been home for about four days. The owner freaked out because she hadn't heard from me and went to my room to see if my stuff was still there. She then decided to search my belongings and found some rolling papers that had been in the bottom of one of my bags for five years. She called the family I used to stay with whom I had used for a reference. She told them I was using drugs, was late on my rent and she was going to evict me. She said she boxed up my stuff and it was in the garage. She wanted me to come pick it up at night after she got home from work.

I couldn't believe it. I thought that was totally bullshit. The minute I found out, I got in my car, and drove over to the house. I put my key in the lock and it didn't work. She had already changed the locks, so I couldn't get in. I went around the house checking the doors and windows and found a small upper window unlocked. I went into the window like Spiderman. I then went into the garage from the door to the house, opened the garage door and loaded up my stuff.

I had no place to stay, so again, I went back over to my friend's family house. About an hour later, the police showed up and said that I've been accused of breaking and entering. I explained what happened and showed them my stuff still loaded in my car. They seemed to be okay and on the verge of leaving, but then told me there was a warrant out for my arrest from Missouri. The charge was felony check writing, out of Farmington, Missouri, for a bad check. I had no idea what it was for, but I was under arrest. I gave my car keys to my friends and told them I would get hold of them as soon as I knew what was going on.

The check I had written for my SR 22 filing, for my high-risk insurance after my DUI in Missouri, had bounced. The check was for $154 and the limits to be a misdemeanor was $150. Both my parents tried to talk to the judge and the prosecuting attorney to pay the check and the court costs, but they wouldn't allow it. They were going to extradite me for a $154 bad check.

They had 30 days to come get me or release me. Since I was in a different state, they re-qualified me as a "fugitive in flight". They took me from the 200 man dormitory to an 8-man high risk felon tank. There were some pretty rough guys in there. The first night in there, about 1 AM, a new prisoner came in and took a guy off the top bunk, punched his head in and took his bed. I slept with one eye open from then on.

I sat in jail for about 28 days and then a retired cop and his wife picked me up. They were really nice to me. We had two hours to talk on the drive from Bakersfield to the LA airport. They took the handcuffs off me, when we went in to McDonald's to eat breakfast, so I wouldn't be embarrassed. After talking with me and knowing the truth about the charge, and my parent's attempt to make restitution, I think they felt a little sorry for me. We flew into the St. Louis airport and drove to Farmington, Missouri.

My awesome Mother came to my rescue once again. She met us there. We went before the judge, and she wrote checks for $2,879 to bail me out again. My $154 bad check went to $609 with court costs, then to $2,879. We had to pay all extradition costs, including the two extra days that the sheriff and his wife spent at the amusement parks in the LA area before they picked me up.

I had been clean and sober for over 30 days and I felt pretty good. I was staying with my mom again and decide to get back in the car business. I started working at a local multi-car franchise and started doing pretty good. One week later, I went out to a nightclub with my best friend, and met a beautiful woman that had a good job and was a Christian. We danced all night and started seeing each other. After my second paycheck, I got a week off to go back to Bakersfield to get my car. I got on a plane, spent one night in Bakersfield, and drove almost straight through to Springfield. I was back in five days, clean and sober. It was the longest I had been clean and sober since I was in high school. I felt really good, almost invincible, but that wouldn't last.

Doing Good/Doing Bad

I moved in with my girlfriend and we were doing great together. Her job was steady and stable and I was selling a lot of cars. I changed jobs to another multi-car franchise and was offered a promotion to manager. We had a new Hyundai store and it was selling below projection. I took my excitement level and trained four new salespeople, and we became the number 1 Hyundai store in Missouri.

I had been smoking some pot and drinking on a regular basis. I had a lot of extra money, making $10,000 plus per month, so I started buying cocaine again. My behavior became very erratic, but I was maintaining. A new boss came in and tried to promote me again, but wanted to cut my pay. I didn't agree with his new plan so he fired me. I got a job managing another store and again production soared. I missed a few days work, with no call and no show and lost that job. I got another job as a manager and again, increased sales drastically and was making big money and using lots of drugs.

This company got bought out by one of the top 10 dealer groups in the United States. They felt I needed a bigger store, with a faster pace and higher sales volume. So they flew me to Dallas and Phoenix for interviews. My love of the desert made me select Phoenix for my new job. I was clean for a couple of months and was working 12 to 15 hour days. I was really tired. When it was time to go home, they asked me to stay longer, and on my day off, they would ask me to work and I would say yes.

I was complaining to one of my finance managers about how tired I was and he asked me if I wanted to try some kryptonite? I said what's that, and he said meth, crystal meth, or methamphetamine. I had done some years before, so I said why not? I was hooked with one snort. With cocaine usage, I almost always could sleep and get some rest before going to work the next day. But with meth, I could stay awake for days, if I wanted to.

I had been doing very good work. Using methamphetamine was exhausting. My productivity started dwindling, and I started falling asleep at work and lost my job within 60 days. I had started using a network marketing product called Vitamist and started selling it and building a business full time. I had been in many network marketing deals over the years and really liked the products. Being an engineer, I understood the pay plans and could really see the ability to make a lot of money, if you worked at it really hard. I had been in Amway, NuSkin, Moly Black Gold, Eagle Shield, etc. If it could be sold through network marketing, I had tried it from nutrition to insulation to oil. I went in full tilt. I borrowed 10 grand from my brother and started spending money on marketing and pushing it 16 hours a day. I was also using a lot of drugs. I became one of the top distributors in the United States almost overnight and started making good money. Then the company changed the pay plan, crapped everybody out, and my dream started spiraling downward. I had put everything I had into this. My income dwindled and I ran out of cash. My dream of financial freedom was destroyed and I had put everything I had in it. Another **void/loss.**

I was very upset. I had been using a lot of drugs. I didn't know if I had been misplacing them by hiding them or what? So I decide to try to stop using. I stayed clean for about a week. I would get a job selling cars, and I would sell 10 to 15 cars in a week or two, so the bosses loved me. I would ask for a cash advance and they would give it to me immediately. I would buy drugs and disappear, make excuses and come back if I had a job. Some would let me do it again and some would just fire me.

I tried to get out of the car business. I needed a job where I didn't have to pass a urine test. I was really good at interviewing. I could stay clean a couple of days, wake up, cleanup and interview for 2-5 jobs a day and get them all. I would accept them and then try one or two, and if it didn't pan out or pay quick enough, I would dump them. I had 47 jobs in one year. I didn't go to all of them, but I was hired for all of them.

In May, 1998, I started driving a cab because it would pay cash daily, and I was doing a good job. I enjoyed the people most of the time and I was staying clean from drugs. I picked up a guy that asked if he could hire me for the next five hours. I told him "sure, no problem" and told him the price. After about an hour, I heard sizzling in the backseat, and I turned around and he was smoking a short glass tube. I freaked out and asked him what he was doing. I thought he was smoking heroin or something. He apologized and said he thought I was cool. He said it was crack or cocaine. I didn't know what crack really was and he explained. It was pre-prepared cocaine ready to smoke. I told him no and the voice inside my head started talking to me. The next thing I knew, I pulled over and asked for a hit. I had forgotten what it felt like to freebase coke. This was a little different, very compact, and very easy and I wasn't hooked on methamphetamine any more. I was hooked on crack, with one hit. I lost my job as a cab driver very shortly after this for erratic driving behavior. I fell asleep at a stoplight, with a fare in the backseat, driving them to work one morning.

I finally got a job selling cars at a "buy here, pay here" lot that didn't require a drug test. It was pretty fun. I could wear shorts and tennis shoes and use drugs. Everyone that came to the store had bad credit. So I could be really pushy and get away with it. Erratic behavior was okay as long as I was selling cars. I sold 54 cars, one month, but only 32 got financed.

During this time, my younger brother JT had gotten in some big trouble. I felt very responsible for his drug problems because I made him get high when he was in the 7th grade, along with his best friend. I did this because I didn't want him to tell on me if he saw me doing it.

His drug use had made him unemployable for a very long time. He was a natural born salesman, like me and my dad. He could sell anything, but was always looking for the bigger and better deal. He had a small possession charge in Texas years before, and then got in trouble in Missouri. Without going into detail, he didn't show up for sentencing and fled the state.

One day, I was at work and a man and a woman walked in and asked for James Mosby. That was my first name, and no one called me that, everyone called me Grady. They identified themselves as federal marshals and asked me if I had seen JT. I told them that I had and that he had showed up here, about three weeks ago, looking for a job. He was a master carpenter, and my boss needed a building constructed for storage on the back of the lot. I told him my brother was an expert, and he gave him a bid and started to work. He was done in about 10 days and he left. I told them I hadn't seen him since, but they didn't believe me. They threw me in the back of a panel van with two other guys and started interrogating me, with the air conditioning off, in the middle of the summer. They showed up about every two days for about 2 to 3 weeks, and repeated the same interrogation. JT called me once in a while, and I told them about their abuse.

The Marshalls followed me home every night from work, which made my drug pickups very nerve-racking. I would have to lose them on a regular basis. They followed me home one night and knocked on my door right after I got home. They pushed their way inside and walked into every room. I'm pretty sure that they put a bug on my phone, and several of my rooms. It could've been my paranoia, but I did hear beeping on the line. After a couple months, they disappeared, when JT was arrested in south Phoenix. I was relieved, and shortly thereafter lost my job selling cars.

I met a guy that owned a male dance team that performed at local bars 3 to 5 nights a week. I became the promotional manager and worked the ladies in the crowd. I sold specialty dances and did light table dances for tips. It was great for cash every night, to fuel my drug habit.

I started stealing from my wife on a regular basis. She was going to night school, to get a computer degree to get a better job and to probably stay away from me. I would steal a check from her and fill it out, sign her name and cash it. I would take money to buy groceries and keep the change to buy drugs. Things were getting really bad. She was a nervous wreck, and I was whacked out. The self-loathing I felt from continually screwing up and not being able to stay clean made me not even want to try.

Second death — HELL

Typical deal, I had been trying to get a good hit for hours. It was too much of a paranoid situation in the apartment. I would see shadows every time I tried to take a hit. I kept thinking my wife would come home and she was going to catch me. It was close to time for her to get home so I tried to straighten up. As soon as she got home I made an excuse for an errand or something and left with my pipe and dope.

I tried a couple spots to see if anyone was home so I could get high safely. Finally, as I was driving through a grocery store parking lot, I saw a chick I'd met before, named Jill. She was with her boyfriend, Jeff on their bikes. I asked if they wanted to get high and they agreed. I loaded up their bikes in my Celica and we headed to their house, which was close by.

We got to their place and it was a small cube of the house; about 600 square ft., a real dive, but it should work. I had never been there before, so I didn't know what to expect. I walked into a small living area that doubled as the kitchen and dining area. Off the back area were two small bedrooms and a half bath with shower.

I had to check the place out first, which kind of freaked them out because they weren't high yet. The bedroom on the left wasn't lived in and was full of junk, boxes and furniture, etc. The backdoor to this room and was slightly ajar, because they had a break-in once, and it was broken. This was a bummer because it filled me with paranoia, quick.

They wanted to use their pipe, which was fine with me because I knew mine was saturated with the unburned dope from the many times I tried to get high all day. It was also common for "tweakers" to want to use their own pipe to do other people's drugs, because of the residue left over that they could use later.

So I called "first hit" and they got the candle ready to light the pipe off of. I prepared my torch (cotton ball around a short metal wire) and poured the 151 rum into a shot glass. I instructed them to get ready to blow out the torch when I was done so the place wouldn't catch on fire, if I got off too good. Plus, I didn't want getting it out to ruin my buzz.

It was a good hit and paranoia started taking over. I got each of them high quickly so they wouldn't be bothered by my glancing looks around. We had several hits and were very high. I then said I wanted to use my pipe. I waited till Jill was ready to assist me by blowing out the torch. I added a good-sized rock to the already saturated pipe. I let my breath out and slowly melted the rock into the screen. I blew out my breath again and very slowly started to inhale. I knew it was going to be a good huge hit and continued a deep breath, filling my lungs full. I motioned for Jill to blow out the torch and she took it and the pipe away from me, and I started getting off.

I thought "Oh No!" and, "Oh my God!", as I started seeing very clear dark shadowy figures beginning to line the whole room, walls from the ground to the ceiling, and sides of doorways. They were looking around from the sides of the doors in the back rooms and bathroom. I started to motion to Jill and Jeff, and speak to them to tell them to "Look out, there they are!" and everything went black.

It felt like a very long time, and I felt my body accelerating downward fast and a heard a huge rumbling. The rumbling reminded me of the sound I had experienced when I was

16 years old, when my family drove to Huntsville, Alabama to see my relatives. This was the summer trip that we drove down to visit them and get a car from them. A beautiful 1966 Chrysler Imperial, all electric, awesome boat. The second day we were there, I took my little brother out for a drive in the late afternoon in our new car, and we got really high on pot. My uncle got home from work about 6:30 and sat down for a drink. He was a senior engineer at Wiley Laboratories. The company was responsible for testing steam release valves for the nuclear power industry. He knew that I was planning on graduating early and going to his alma mater, the University of Missouri-Rolla engineering school, to study nuclear engineering. He got a call from work and was called to go back because they were having problems. He poured some bourbon into a cup of coffee and said to me, "Let's go".

I was really high, as he spoke to me about what to expect. Someone hadn't marked a bad part that they used over again, and they had a radiation spike in their power area. He had to monitor the radiation cleanup and make sure they got back on schedule. We arrived at the location, and there was a long walkway down to the work area in a big open field, in front of two huge electric steam generators. These generators powered the steam generation, to simulate pressures in a nuclear power facility. They caused the ground to vibrate and rumble. The noise was so intense it filled my body and ears to the point of needing earplugs.

That was just like this noise, huge, shocking, rumbling and roaring. Then "whoosh", a feeling of downward acceleration and then slow movement. The rumbling could still be heard in the background. My vision around me seemed dark and deep blood wine red all around, with the smell of sulfur smoke burning my nostrils. I heard cracking like whips and chains. I heard sharp, loud, guttural barking voices that sounded like the language of the Middle East, Arabic or some kind of foreign language. In the distance I saw mountains and valleys, and a lake that seem to be on fire. There appeared to be thousands of other figures in motion, in the valleys below. The masses appeared to be in sync to the cracking of the whips and shouting.

All of a sudden, it felt like chains started slapping me around from all directions and wrapping up my body. Then I felt a burning searing pain in my midsection. I didn't understand what had happened until I looked down and saw I was missing all of my male parts. I had been castrated and a feeling of hopelessness took over. I had lost my identity, helpless. I'd been made a eunuch, and my masculinity taken away from me.

I noticed different types of grotesque, mutilated figures starting to come in contact with me. One flying thing had a huge mouth, big teeth and a grotesque head with a very small body and wings. It would buzz around me, snapping its teeth at me trying to bite me and making a terrible noise. Another, I remember was very similar in looks, but it had a body and was missing an arm and I didn't notice any wings but it was trying to pull at me and bite me in the same way as the winged creature. There were other demon-like creatures, with wings, buzzing me and trying to bite my arms and my shoulder socket. They were fighting each other, as if competing to get first in line to get at me. I thought they were trying to take parts of my body to replace theirs.

I could see in my peripheral vision, a very large creature with horns on his head with a whip, cracking it and shouting out commands in a foreign language. As the creatures got closer and continued to bite at my body, I felt like I had lost a part of my shoulder socket, and it was coming apart at the joint. I felt a searing pain in my legs and I started praying, "Our Father, which Art in Heaven, hallowed be Thy Name. Thy kingdom come, Thy Will be done, on earth as it is in heaven". I was gasping and crying in searing pain and somehow continued, "give us this day our daily bread and forgive us our trespasses as we forgive those who trespass against us, and lead us not into temptation but deliver us from evil", then whoosh, my body accelerating... I came to, gagging on the ground with Jeff looming over me, yelling at me to chill out.

I asked him what he was doing on top of me, and he said I had passed out, turned blue and quit breathing. He'd been giving me mouth-to-mouth until I started breathing. He told me to get the f—- out. I grabbed my bag and left shaking and crying.

I got home and my wife asked what happened. I told her, I was so sorry and that I had overdosed and died. I don't know how she really felt but she looked horrified. My heart was palpitating with an irregular beat for hours. I cried on the couch for hours.

The "Lord's Prayer" had saved my life. When Jesus' disciples asked him how they should pray, he had taught them this prayer. It makes sense that we have everything in it, that anyone would ever need. When I had said, "deliver us from evil," its power delivered me, to save my life and God pulled me out of hell.

I came to believe later that when you go to hell, they take away your identity first. In the case of a man, they castrate you immediately. Then they take away every part of physical beauty that you ever held onto in this beautiful world we live in. They disfigure you and make you a horrible wasted piece of flesh, which you have to spend eternity trying to remake, to some form of your old self. Or who knows...

My wife smelled the foul smoke on me when I got home that day, and I smelled it in my nostrils for days. It was a sulfur smoke smell like I'd never smelled before. It was much worse than the sulfur smell in the oil fields that I was used to working in. I had multiple bite marks on my shoulder area, and my kneecaps had bite mark bruises that stayed for days.

After I got clean and sober, I became very good friends

with a pastor of an old church I used to attend, who told his story about visiting the lake of fire in hell. When he was a very young man, he had a dream, or it was a vision, where he was transported to hell and looked over the lake of fire. He talked about the smell and how when he came back he smelled it for days. This was the turning point when he decided to become a pastor.

Hell is terrible, hell exists, and I know I don't want to ever be there again. I was given a second chance, and I really didn't want to screw it up again.

Busted

I stayed clean for about a week and I started feeling better. I started to clean, to throw away paraphernalia and I found needles and old pipes. I threw away the needles but not the pipes. I got high from scraping residue off a couple of old pipes I found. I was "chasing the Dragon" again.

It was September 17, 1997. When my wife got home I had planned to go get pizza and get enough change, along with the couple bucks that I had, to go to my crack dealer and get a dime rock and get back to the house quick. I told my wife to give me a couple extra bucks to get some sodas and bolted out the door, heading for the Roosevelt area, where I scored my drugs. I pulled up behind the house, where I had been buying lately.

Strangely enough, a white guy answered the door and asked me what I wanted. Mexicans usually ran these crack houses. They were disposable. I told him I was looking for the Mexican guy and he coaxed me in and asked what I wanted. I hesitated and then told him I wanted a 10 spot, and he tried to force his hand toward me with something that looked like a macadamia nut. It was obviously not cocaine. As I was pulling back my hand with the $10 bill, several big white guys burst out of the back bedroom and rushed me. They slammed me into the door and kept me on the ground. They took me into the back room and there sat the Mexican guys, all sitting on the ground handcuffed, waiting to be taken to jail.

The police had set up a sting operation to bust users. I assume it was to stop traffic in the area and find out about other informants, to inform on other drugs locations. On a positive note, it was also used for helping people get help for their drug problems. I remember a police officer talking with me, after they shuttled us to another base camp of operations they had set up at another business nearby, where they were processing us. He told me that they would help me get clean.

Fortunately, Arizona has a program like some other states, called drug diversion. If it was your first felony offense for drugs, you could get it reduced to a misdemeanor with the completion of several months of drug outpatient counseling along with random urine testing and monthly appearances in drug court. Drug court, is where the judge reviews your progress and allows you to go to the next level, and to completion; if you stay clean.

I did pretty well in the first several months of the program. The experience of the seven days in jail scared me straight. I had to call in daily to a number to see if my color came up. Daily, a color was on a recording for probation people to call. If it was your color, you had to go and piss test. I got a job, was making my nightly meetings and things were good at home.

I went to my drug court evaluation and got moved up to the next level. I started getting a paycheck, and then I bought some dope to get high and my color came up the next day. I didn't go pee, because I knew I couldn't pass. So I was on the lamb. Drug court was in two weeks, a bench warrant for my arrest would be issued and I would be arrested, if caught. A bench warrant was issued for my arrest on September 25, 1998.

I knew I was in big trouble and I needed to get some help. I knew I had to have some documentation of an inpatient program, showing I was trying to get some help, if I was going to keep out of jail. I had enough experience with hospitals to know that they wouldn't admit me on my wife's insurance for cocaine addiction, so I went to a local hospital and told them I wanted to commit suicide. I stayed in for several days and then checked myself out.

With a bench warrant from drug court, the police didn't come looking for you, because they knew you would screw up eventually. Addiction just gets worse, especially with failure when trying to get clean. The guilt of the relapse causes the addict to medicate and fill the void deeper and deeper, so he takes more risks, trying to get higher "chasing the Dragon". The Bible says; "when a man's house is cleaned and the devil leaves, he goes all about looking for a dirty house to live in but then if he comes back and sees the house is clean, he will bring seven more of his buddies, even worse than he is, to stay" (paraphrased). I think that is why it gets so bad and the guilt feels worse. Failing yourself and letting everyone else down you love, really makes you feel you have nothing left to lose. It creates a 'void' that you fill with self-loathing and despair.

Sure enough, December 7, 1998, I had just dropped off my wife at work and was heading to score. I jumped on the freeway on ramp and must've sped by a motorcycle cop. He pulled me over for speeding before I even got on the freeway. He ran me for warrants and off to jail I went. Don't pass go!

Part of drug court was, if you screwed up, you got a series of other chances. If you couldn't do drug court, you had to complete the balance of 60 days in jail. You got to experience the good life (ha ha). I had 53 days left to serve since I had been jailed seven days previously. Then, I would go on regular probation. So off to jail I went, to spend it during Christmas and New Year's Eve, at the famous tent city.

For the first few days, while getting processed, they put me in a huge room with probably 200+ bunk beds. They do this until they figure out where each guy is going after their initial court visits. I was there for about a week. The second night I was there, I had this miracle visitation in a dream. This dream was in vivid color. I saw Jesus, with open arms standing at the end of the table facing me. He had a flowing robe that radiated behind him in all directions. His light brown hair was flowing like a mane. He had a golden halo above his head that had rays radiating out from it. He had brilliant blue eyes and penetrating smile, and he spoke; "Come to Me".

I woke up bawling like a baby. The guy in the bunk above me came down to comfort me and told me it was going to be all right. I told him about the dream and he cried too. I cried hard for about an hour. I had to get clean. I had to get some real help.

You may have heard of "tent city" designed by our famous Sheriff Joe Arpaio. It was designed to save taxpayers money. Military tents were erected in the field outside of the main jail to house inmates. You may have heard stories about how cold it gets at night in the desert. If you were lost, without a way to keep warm, you could freeze to death. In the day time it was in the 70's and sunny, and at night in the 20's and 30's. We were allowed only one blanket. So when people were released, we would scavenge their blanket and make up our bed really tight, so the guards wouldn't notice. This was the only way we could stay warm at night. We were told not to sneak leftover food to our bunks because of mice. I thought that sounded funny, but you could hear them eating every night. It would drive me crazy.

I got out the first part of February feeling pretty good. I had started reading my Bible every day and going to jail house AA/NA meetings. When I got home, I quit reading my Bible. My wife had to move us to a new apartment while I was in jail. She left our waterbed and remaining furniture in the old apartment. All we had was a bed, small kitchen table and a TV. She bought some blowup furniture for the living room.

I stayed clean for about three weeks, then I used again. I told my wife. She was crushed. I told her I would see my probation officer and ask for help. I met with my probation officer and told him I needed some inpatient treatment. I told him I tried to use insurance to get into the hospital but they wouldn't accept it for cocaine addiction. In order to use insurance at the hospital, I had to be an alcoholic or heroin addict or feeling suicidal. I told him I needed a 30 day program, and he gave me the name of several.

I checked into place called El Corazon. It was a nice clean facility. It consisted of several old brick duplexes for housing. It had a main office and a central building where we ate and had meetings. We would get up early and by 7 AM did exercises, then ate breakfast. We had eight hours of classes with a break for lunch and meetings at night. There were four men to a room. I stayed two weeks. I decided I had the AA recovery thing figured out and left. I knew I could do it on my own now.

That lasted about 10 days, and then I was using again. I didn't want to lose my wife. I knew if I didn't get clean, I would be going **back** to jail, get hurt or maimed from overdosing and falling down, busting my face, getting paralyzed or worse. I wasn't afraid of dying. **I almost wanted to die**, the guilt was so strong.

Desperation

I t was the same thing all over again. I would pawn the TV for cash to get high. My wife would get paid and get it out of pawn, and I would do it again. One night, I was very loaded, and I was hiding in the back bedroom. My wife knew I was in there getting high, freaking out so she threatened to call the police. I didn't blame her. She was so sick and tired of it. I left the apartment and went and hid on the balcony. They found me and I started to run. The police tackled me and held me down, while the paramedics tried to examine me. I was delirious, so they put me on a gurney, attached an IV and took me to the hospital. My heart rate was going crazy on the monitor, bleep bleep bleep bleep. They thought I was going to die. They treated me and in the morning, I checked myself out and walked to my drug dealer's house.

I took it easy and stayed high for the next few days. I got some sleep and woke up the next morning and stole a check from my wife. I waited for her to leave for work, and got in my car. I went to the check cashing store to cash a forged check for $40. I headed to the crack house, and then home. I made sure all the curtains were closed, doors locked, and I started getting high. My paranoia was so strong. I got a good first hit and had trouble from then on.

Something appeared to me in the right side of my vision, and it spoke to me. I told it I was so miserable and tired of screwing up all the time. The vision told me that when people die they become angels, and then they can help watch over their loved ones. I decided it was better for me to be dead and help my wife and family from heaven, instead of hurting them with my actions here on earth.

So I wrote this letter:

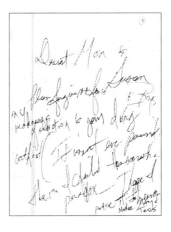

Dearest, Susan and mom, LJ, JT, family and friend, I have wronged you in my long life of selfishness. I'm sorry. Please forgive me.

Dearest, mom, Susan and boys, Please forgive me for my weakness of addiction and your doing without (it wasn't ever/even planned). The more I failed the worst the paradox. I hope I make it to heaven.

Mother Mary and Jesus please forgive me, so I can meet my angels and baby Shannon (my dead twin brother who died at nine months old).

Please don't feel bad. You have truly helped me live a fun life. Mom the dope has altered my brain to mental illness. My failure is not your fault, and thanks for making me go to church and your pure love.

Please pray out loud for God to allow my forgiveness for my final chance to live with Shannon and granddad in heaven so I can hug you when you get there.

Believe and pray out loud for your angels to guide path in all you desire and need. Don't feel remorseful. I am on your right shoulder always. Speak my name for advice to guide you. That's how I'll make it up to all of you for your material sacrifice and emotional pain. Please don't forget this!! Tell everyone. Don't be quiet! You deserve every pleasure. Don't be unselfish! Please allow me to be forgiven, from heaven by asking <u>out loud</u> *"Grady in the name of God, the father and the Holy Ghost, please guide my request for ＿＿＿ ＿＿＿ ＿＿＿. Pray your choice and fill in the blanks, have fellowship of the church/tithes with men of God in conjunction with the word and power of prayer (This came to me in a vision of how to be allowed to enter heaven).*

The pain I've created has had its course. Please forgive me, I'm sorry, it wasn't personal, LJ, JT, boys, all of you. I've loved you with all my breaking heart. Please heal yours, due to me. Sorry, my brain was altered (if only you knew).

Just say no to drugs. It showed me heaven on my first

*near-death overdose and saved me from hell, as they fought
over parts of my body, no sex, castration as they first make
you a eunuch.*

*No guilt, talk, keep the temple clean. Praise Jesus and
Mother Mary for eternal life at God's side.*

*Please help allow my way God has given me to repent.
Pray for me in the next three days and talk to God through
me and I'll guide you.*

*Have fun life carefree sacrifice, giving mom lottery
(?????) Whoever, whatever you ask for*

I love you all G.

That was my suicide letter. I left it on the kitchen counter
and then turned the A/C off. I took two lighters and went to
the back bedroom, which had a small bathroom with a single
toilet and I closed the door. I had already turned off the AC
so there wouldn't be any wind to blow out the flame. I closed
the door to minimize any shadows around windows, door
edges or doorways that could mess up my concentration or
get in the way of getting a good hit, my final hit. I knew it
could be the one that would kill me, if I got it right, because
the pipe was saturated, and I was about to put a huge amount
of cocaine in it.

I started to light the pipe and my first lighter lit, but kept
going out. It was full, but wasn't working for some reason. I
switched to the other lighter, but it would hardly stay lit long
enough to start to melt the huge rock. It would start to light,
and then go out. Then the wheel that was used to ignite the
flame broke off, as if it had gotten too hot and had melted.

I was pissed off. I opened the door and went back to the
kitchen. I got an almost full book of matches and another
with three matches left in it and went back in the bathroom. I
tried to light the matches and put them up to the first lighter
to ignite it, as I pushed the fuel lever, nothing came out. I
switched to trying to set up matches to light my hit. To be

effective, I knew I had to have several sets of 2-3 together to light long enough and hot enough to burn the cocaine properly. Every time I tried to light the pipe, a wisp of wind continued to blow out the matches. I heard a big voice yell **"NO!"** It freaked me out so bad, I started crying and hit my knees and started thanking God for saving my life again. It was not my time to die yet.

I realized later that the "father of lies", the devil; had tried to trick me into coming to death with him to Hades. I had forgotten the lesson from my second near-death experience. I had learned that if I overdosed and died, I would be going to hell.

Also, after analyzing the suicide letter, I noticed the reference to mother Mary. I am not Catholic, so in my rational mind, I wouldn't have prayed to Mary. So it made me realize even more, that this was the demonic attempt to send me straight to hell.

I had to get some real help. I flushed my drugs down the toilet. I broke my glass pipe and flushed it too. I turned on the AC and the TV, then lay on the bed and waited for my wife to get home. I told her what had happened, and she was appalled. I told her I would talk to my probation officer and ask him if I could try to get into the Salvation Army Adult Rehabilitation Center for Men (ARC).

Two days later, I talked to my probation officer again in desperation, and told him what had happened. I had researched a couple of free six-month programs and I wanted mine to be Christian based. I asked him if I could have one more chance to get clean. He said he would check with the judge and let me know. I left feeling hopeful, and I got the call several hours later that I could check into the Salvation Army Adult Rehab Center for Men. It would save my life.

Salvation/Rebirth

The news was awesome. I felt so hopeful, but I really needed my wife to make the phone call to get me in. I had called about the program several months earlier, when I was trying to get inpatient help, but some weird force kept me from picking up the phone myself. She was a little disturbed by being forced to do something for my recovery, probably because of all the previous failed attempts, but she did it anyway. I'm sure she did it to help, but also to give her some peace.

She called the local facility in Phoenix, and we were told they were all booked up. They were full for the next few weeks. My heart plummeted, but they said, that it might be possible to get into the location in Tucson, only 100 miles south of Phoenix. That would probably be better anyway. It was a good distance from home, so maybe I wouldn't just walk out and expect to come home.

She called work and got the next day off, and I packed my bags. Like several times before, when I had a geographical (move to change location, associations and connections), my life fit into two suitcases and two large boxes. I also had a small rock and a couple of pinches of pot I snuck into the car. We packed the car with my bags and my dog Vinnie, and headed for Tucson.

We checked into a crappy Motel 6 type motel and settled

in for a long night. I told Susan I had a little pot and I was going to smoke it. I used a Coca-Cola can, smashed one side, and poked several holes in it and proceeded to get high in the bathroom.

She was very irritated. She watched TV and tried to go to sleep. I waited till I had a small cake of ashes across the holes, and I made a feeble attempt to try and melt some of my crack-rock and smoke it slowly. It was just enough to ruin my buzz and make me paranoid. My wife knew I was doing coke, which made her want to call the cops on me.

Before long, the pot and crack were gone and I tried to get some rest. Sunrise came early. My appointment for intake was scheduled at 8:30 AM. Susan got me to the location and helped me get my stuff onto the curb and said "Get well, or don't come home" and drove off. She'd been through more than anybody should ever have to put up with. I went inside to the Salvation Army Adult Rehabilitation Center for men in Tucson, Arizona, with high hopes.

After brief discussion, I took a breathalyzer and had to pee in a clear test container. I proceeded to start filling out more paperwork, which asked for clothing sizes, shirt, shoes and pants, etc. Just as I finished, the head of the department, the house manager told me I couldn't come in yet. My cocaine and marijuana levels were too high and I needed to get clean before entering their clean environment. I explained that's why I was here and I couldn't get clean on the outside. They said they had a halfway house several miles away that I could stay at for the weekend, and we could try again on Monday.

They gave me a ride in one of their vans. I unloaded all of my stuff and took it upstairs, put it under my bed and went to sleep. I slept for 11 hours and was awakened by a guy telling me chow was ready. There was a mix of people, male and female, all homeless for some reason or another. After dinner, the house manager said I could sleep again until tomorrow, and then I'd have to take part in cleaning and church on Sunday. When I got rested and active, I started feeling hopeful again. Monday came around quickly.

Unfortunately, there was no ride back to the ARC, so I had to walk. It was a little less than 3 miles away. Now remember, I had two large suitcases and two large boxes, and I couldn't carry them all. It was already over 90° on this May day in southern Arizona. I began by carrying my two suitcases about 50 yards, and then would walk back and carry the other two boxes. An hour later, at 100+ degrees, I was soaking wet (even with 15% humidity). Cars were driving by me honking and yelling at me. How embarrassing. I finally made it, cold water and air conditioning, the Salvation Army, yeah!

The intake manager made me pee in the cup again and I crossed my fingers as I handed it to him. The desk manager held up a breathalyzer for me. The intake manager came back shaking his head and said I was still dirty, but my levels were way down so I could be admitted.

They took my big boxes to storage and gave me receipts. I took my suitcases to my room and unloaded my clothes and necessities. I didn't realize I didn't need them, because when I filled out my clothing paperwork, it was so I could go next door to the Salvation Army store and buy what I needed. All participants were allowed six shirts and six pants. One pair of dress shoes and one regular pair, underwear, tie and two suit jackets. This was so we could attend mandatory church on Sunday and Wednesday night.

I wanted a Christian-based program, because I was raised in the Methodist Church. My mother always took us to Sunday school. Even when we were in junior high and high school, she made us go even though I yelled and cussed at her sometimes, not wanting to go. I knew in my heart that God could heal my addiction, if I gave it all up to Jesus.

This program understood the basics of fallen man, no motivation, no belonging, no organization, and no stable life patterns. So the first thing we discussed in the orientation was the schedule. Breakfast was from 6 to 7:30 AM. Our bed had to be made before we went to breakfast, and we had to be showered and shaved.

All men had to work to be fed and to stay in the program. The ARC was attached to the main Tucson warehouse for incoming donations to the Salvation Army. The first job everyone had was sorting clothes. We separated the good from the bad, and then hung them on hangers. The loose items, purses, belts, shoes, we sorted and tagged with prices. We broke at noon for a 30 to 45 minute lunch, then back to work till 5 PM. Then, we got a chance to get cleaned up and dinner was from 5:30 to 6:30. We had AA classes every night. On Wednesday night, we dressed up for the evening church service, with singing and sermon. Saturday was our day off, and Sunday we dressed up for church again, with a great service and a good dinner.

At the end of every week, we received an allowance for the canteen. The first week it was five dollars. The next week, six dollars and a dollar more each week until it reached $20. It stayed $20 per week until graduation. The third day I was there, I asked this guy, Darren, where I could get a Bible to start reading. He said he would ask the chaplain and 10 minutes later he brought me one of his old ones and told me to keep it. I wanted to be like my granddad and start learning about God. Like a workout routine, I started my day getting up early and reading the Old/New Testament. I wanted to start learning a new way to handle my life. Darren had been in for three months, and one month later he pulled out early. He had relapsed.

The next Monday I was asked if I wanted to schedule time with the chaplain. His name was Floyd. I said yes, and the next day I was taken out of work at 1 PM and went to Floyd's office. Floyd had completed the ARC program. He had been in the mortgage business before making big money. The cash, girls, drugs, all caught up with him and he lost everything.

We talked a little while longer, and I told him a little about my background, parents, and my life during drug decline. He then asked me if I was ready to accept Jesus back into my life and let God take control. I said yes and he asked me to recite the "Sinner's prayer" I recited.....................

"Dear God in heaven, I come to you in the name of Jesus. I acknowledge to You that I am a sinner, and I am sorry for my sins and the life that I have lived; I need your forgiveness.

I believe that your only begotten Son Jesus Christ shed His precious blood on the cross at Calvary and died for my sins, and I am now willing to turn from my sin.

You said in Your Holy Word, Romans 10:9 that if we confess the Lord our God and believe in our hearts that God raised Jesus from the dead, we shall be saved.

Right now I confess Jesus as the Lord of my soul. With my heart, I believe that God raised Jesus from the dead. This very moment I accept Jesus Christ as my own personal Savior and according to His Word, right now I am saved.

Thank you, Jesus, for dying for me and giving me eternal life.
Amen. "

Then all of a sudden, whoosh, a feeling of sudden acceleration came up out of my body like a huge rush of pain, remorse, despair, fear, anger - all removed in the rush of the wind. I cried that deep, uncontrollable crying, that tore at the very bottom of my stomach like it had before. The crying was like the time Jesus came to me in my dream in jail and the two times I died and came back from seeing heaven and hell. It was also like the time when I was a little boy and my mom told me my parents were getting a divorce.

The guilt had been removed. So now, all I had to do was start working on me.

During the first 30 days. There were no outside phone calls, visits or contact. It worried me that my wife would leave me if I wasn't there to control it. But then I realized I wasn't controlling it for many years. So I hunkered down and did my program. After 30 days phone calls were allowed in the evening after dinner. We could go to the outside AA meetings to see other groups and get a sponsor. After 90 days; we could get a weekend pass and I got to spend it with Susan and our dog Vinnie, which gave me strength to carry on. I was finally heading in the right direction, and I had started making amends wherever I could.

When I arrived, I had been on medication for my anxiety and depression, Paxil and Xanax. I started to pray for healing of my depression symptoms and was able to wean myself off of Paxil and Xanax, within a couple weeks.

God started blessing me immediately. It was just like Joseph being placed in the pharaoh's jail, then moving to a job in the jailer's household; I got moved up to a dispatch job after the first four weeks. My job was to route trucks and take calls on donations. I met a driver who brought in Mexican cigarettes. I started buying them and selling them to the guys who smoke. We were not allowed to work when we were in the program, but they allowed guys to buy cigarettes from each other. I started practicing tithing with my weekly allowance and with my cigarette profits. I even started make child support payments while still in the program, making amends where I could and asking for forgiveness in areas where I couldn't.

November 1999, I graduated into my new life, as a new person, so I could begin to live and love. I got my respect back from my wife, my twin boys and my family. I had racked up a lot of debt with my usage of drugs. My prayer had been for the "miracle of debt cancellation" and God blessed me with that. Like the Israelites when they left Egypt, God had told them to ask for wealth from the Egyptians, and they showered it upon them. Just like the fish producing the two coins for Peter to pay the Temple back for himself and Jesus. I even paid off my back child support and delinquent student loan debt from college.

I bought my first house, and the Lord blessed my income to begin making 2 to 4 times more than any other salesperson. I started paying extra on the house and got it paid off in 7-1/2 years. Like Job in the Bible, when the devil took away his life, he was faithful and got it back many times over. God was blessing me. All the promises of AA/NA were true.

It says in James 5:19-20; "My brothers, if one of you should wander from the truth and someone should bring him back, remember this: Whoever turns a sinner from the error of his way will save him from death and cover over a multitude of sins."

Now, my new prayer is to share my near-death experience with the world. So people can know **there is a Heaven and there is a Hell**. They are real, and you don't want to end up in Hell. The voids and the losses we experience in life's path and in our choices; need to be filled with the love of God. That's why we were made. Filling our pains with the easy quick fixes the world provides, lust, greed, drugs, overeating, etc. can only end up in near-death.

God loves you, and is waiting for you with open arms. I love you and good luck.

"Family photo with twin boys and grandchildren"

Conclusions

I am not a counselor. I'm only a man who has learned from his experiences. Please don't take offense at anything I'm about to say.

Take it easy on yourself. You don't have to do it alone. I pray that God will heal any situation you are going through. God is madly and hopelessly in love with you.

1) Parents—we all love our children. When your children have failures/losses through activities or relationships, please talk with them and let them know they are loved. Encourage them and help them find other hobbies/activities to fill their pathway or to continue in their current activities. Make sure you spend some quality time talking about how their failures make them feel. Do this so they won't suffer feelings of failure/loss that they might stuff with other negative activities of this world to make them feel better (drugs, alcohol, sex, anger, over eating, depression, hurting themselves or others, etc.)

Fill their situations of failure with positive influences, when they are let down or when their desires are not met immediately (self-help programs, Bible reading, professional counseling, etc.)

Failures/voids/losses are a big deal for children and they need to be talked about. People need fulfillment and they will seek it anyway they can.

The world our children are growing up in it so different from the one we grew up in. Everything is immediate satisfaction, from immediate text response, to fast food and DVR's getting rid of commercials. Children aren't talking, they are texting. We need to protect them the best we can. We need to protect them and take them to church. You don't have to go until you are ready, just take them. Churches have lots of children and young adult programs that are fun. The information I learned saved my life. My mother gave birth to me twice by teaching me about Jesus. When I was dead, all I had to do was ask and I was born again.

2) People struggling with addictions and families of those people—please do whatever it takes to get professional help for addictions or behaviors that are filling your voids and losses.

Life is way too short, to not be able to live it to its fullest. People are very stubborn and self-centered. We think that we can handle our problems on our own. We tell ourselves that emotional pain will go away by itself, if we ignore it. It's just not true.

The guys that started Alcoholics Anonymous knew that people were self-centered. They knew that people with addictive behaviors were stubborn, blaming everyone else for their problems and angry at others, themselves and God. So the basis, of the program, requires the recovering addict or alcoholic to admit they have a problem and that they couldn't fix it on their own. Then they were to ask their higher power, as they know it, to help them. This would enable the self-centered human, to not reject the program based on religion or God.

Religion may have disappointed many of you and driven you away. Wars fought in the name of God and man using religion to make a lot of money and take from the faithful. It doesn't matter if you believe in Christianity, Islam, Judaism, Hinduism, or Buddhism there is a God, no matter what you want to call it. All you have to do is see a baby born, or hummingbird fly or beautiful sunset or the crashing waves of the ocean and know there is a God. We aren't just here.

People are very stubborn. We will stay in a bad situation for very long time. We will be given many opportunities to change our situation, but procrastinate and stay right where we are at. Like the story in the Bible about Moses and Pharaoh. Time and time again, after each plague, Moses would say to Pharaoh, "Let my people go". Pharaoh would say "wait till tomorrow and I'll give you an answer", instead of saying "yes" when given the opportunity to stop his suffering now. This applies to our relationships, changing jobs, bad habits and behaviors.

People may make comments, and sometimes people with addictive behaviors are led to believe, that addicts are "weak". This is not true! It is just the opposite! To do the things it takes to stay addicted (i.e., steal, manipulate, lie, embarrassment, doing without, risking your life and health, etc.) takes a lot of determination! When that determination is turned around, and committed to recovery, success is right around the corner! So DO NOT give up!!!

The two times I died, I saw heaven the first time and hell the second time. There is a heaven and there is a hell and you don't want to end up in hell. So make a decision today, to get some help, to get on the right track to enjoy life now because the afterlife is really long and you don't want to end up in the wrong place!

Notes

* Sinner's Prayer from Internet source BibleGateway. com, a Ministry of Gospel communications

There are many versions of the "Sinner's Prayer". All that is important is that you acknowledge that Jesus Christ is God's son, and that you believe he died on the cross for our sins, and then on the third day he rose again, so that we could be forgiven from our sins. Admit that you are truly sorry and that you want to repent and be forgiven. Romans 10:9-10

TheFreeDictionary.com and Merriam-Webster.com for definitions of void and loss

**Life Application Bible, New International Version by Zondervan Publishing House, Grand Rapids Michigan, and Tyndale House Publishers, Inc. Wheaton Illinois. Copyright: 1988, 1989, 1990 and 1991.

You can give donations to the Salvation Army for help with rehabilitation programs for men, women and children. They help families in need and disaster situations also. Call 1-800-SAL-ARMY (725-2769) or email to www. salvationarmyusa.org

Join me on my Facebook page at "A Near Death Experience: I Died and Came Back From Hell"

You may email me at: <u>andexperience@hotmail.com</u>

A donation of 5% cents, for each copy sold of "A Near Death Experience: I Died and Came Back From Hell", will be given to the Salvation Army Adult Rehabilitation Center program.

CPSIA information can be obtained at www.ICGtesting.com
Printed in the USA
BVOW080757260313

316434BV00001B/1/P